Poetic Testimony

A Story of God's Hope, Grace, and Provision

Samantha Harvell

BookLeaf Publishing

India | USA | UK

Made with ❤ on the BookLeaf Publishing Platform
www.bookleafpub.in
www.bookleafpub.com

Dedication

To my son, Noah,

Whether mommy is here in a year or fifty years, know
that you can always rely on the Lord Jesus Christ!

I love you dear son, as you're a gift from above,
This Christmas I want you to know, all about Christ's
endless love.

I was led to this very thing to do,
Writing these poems, dedicated just for you.

So much to say, with so little time,
You need to know, Christ is completely Divine.

God entrusted me with a task,
There is no more time to bask.

Jesus is the only way,
To see the Father's kingdom one day.

Many lessons in the struggles we face,
But there surrounding us is always God's grace.

These poems aren't just poetic art,
They were written with a Holy Spirit led heart.

Entrust in the Lord, not things of this world,
God's promises are all written in His Word.

I love you so much, to the moon and beyond,
To show through encouragement, of yours' and Christ's
bond.

Christmas is about God's love,
A baby born, Jesus a symbol of a dove.

Love Always to the moon and back times infinity,
Mommy xoxoxox

Preface

Let's face it, life can be downright overwhelming and hard. However, through the Lord's grace and abundant love, we can rest under the covering of His wing as the Lord's burden is light (Psalm 91:4, Matthew 11:30). I pray these short, poetic testimonies of the Lord's grace upon my life bring hope in despair and peace among chaos. May the Lord Jesus, bless you and keep you!

Acknowledgements

Thank you, Lord, for your grace and provision upon my life! I pray the Lord bless all who read this book and the He can soften many hearts through these poems. In Jesus Name I pray, Amen.

I want to thank my fiancé, Matthew, my sister, Angela, and all family and friends who support my every ambition! I want to also thank everyone for the thoughts and prayers as I continue to face these health difficulties, but know the Lord is good and answers every prayer. I love each and every one of you and hope that this first book will bring you hope regardless of what trials you are facing. Our Lord is so good and precious to each of us, all the time (Psalm 145:9)! God bless you and thank you for your support!

With love,

Sam

Poem 1. A Fight for Life

My darkest hour, a fight for life,
Against cruelty, of sin and strife.

A victim to violence, left to die in despair,
These monsters, didn't care.

Life support humming, not a soothing sound,
Whimpering cries echo, mother hit the ground.

This fragile thread, it must cling,
Hold on to prayer, for healing it'll bring.

Seeking to kill, the agony and pain,
A glimmer of hope, as a gentle refrain.

Thirsting for water, Yehweh there,
Reassured daughter, His repair.

Blind in the dark, a beacon to shine,
Sighting a light, so very divine.

In adversity, His strength prevails,
My soul resilient, His love never fails.

Despite trials, time to persevere,
With grace sufficient, nothing to fear.

Trust in Him, my rock, my guide,
In His grace, I will forever abide.

Poem 2. The Lego Master

The toy box of life, similar to Legos I build,
Lessons from mistakes, my spirit's filled.

Looking up, big green eyes so wide,
The Master, He is who I confide.

His guidance so gentle, with love so pure,
The Master teaches, His grace is sure.

The path is rocky, the road quite narrow,
But Jesus is the living arrow.

Mistakes made, they don't define,
My child within, continuing to shine.

Through the eyes of the Master,
I am not a total disaster.

Eyes truly opened, I can see,
Loving Master, here to set me free.

Learning from an innocent heart,
Like that of child, Jesus set them apart.

Poem 3. A Delicate Dance

Among the chaos, we must find a way,
Navigate adversity, day by day.

Rasing a son, a scared task,
Weathering storms, no time to bask.

Co-parenting, delicate dance,
Tiptoeing, constant prance.

Compromise and communication, these are key,
Keep focus on our son, he's most important you see.

But the black of night,
We find a guiding light.

The name, of Jesus we find,
Transforming power, any heart and mind.

The narcissist's heart, once hard and cold,
Finding new paths, out with the old.

Grace and forgiveness, the journey begins,
Towards a future, free life's sins.

Poem 4. Blessed With a Sister

Blessed with a sister, she's a friend so dear,
Through joy and sadness, she's always near.

In joy, in sorrow,
Her advice, I borrow.

Secrets and stories, our bond very strong,
Among her presence, I feel I always belong.

Sending a lifeline, when I feel drowned,
Her comforting words, a soothing sound.

Through thick and thin, we've laughed and cried,
But we are always, by each other's side.

Her kindness and compassion, they have no end,
My sister is my confidante, and my forever friend.

I'm so grateful, her never-ending love,

I'm pretty sure, she's a gift from above.

Blessed with a sister, she's so true,
Praising the Lord for, giving me you.

Poem 5. I Didn't Know Love

I didn't know love, God gave me a son,
He's a precious gift, my heart forever won.

Laughter like music, a smile so bright,
In my son's eyes, I see the purest light.

Vow to protect, in all my might,
For with God, everything's alright.

He's a gift, from the great I AM,
Shepherd my, gentle little lamb.

With every step, filled with such pride,
For my son, I'll conquer a tide.

A wonderful creation, a gift from above,
Can't halt it, mother's never-ending love.

Child so pure, and so true,
My son's innocence, my faith anew.

Teaching right from wrong, He'll show the way,
Through darkest moments, Jesus will be your ray.

Cherish every moment, every smile and tear,
My precious son, Jesus is always near.

My son reminds, of God's love and grace,
I cherish snuggle, his every tiny embrace.

Hold him close and never let go,
Seed to plant and watch it grow.

I didn't know love, God gave me a son,
He's a precious gift, my heart forever won.

Poem 6. The Very Breath of Life

Breathless, struggling to survive,
Gasping, a desperate drive.

Respiratory failure, the silent foe,
Septic shock, an additional blow.

The Ultimate Physician, giving all my hope,
Miraculous healing, beginning to cope.

Battling darkness, to end the strife,
Yehweh is, the very breath of life.

Fragile moments, a dance with fate,
Healer's touch, a chance to create.

Poem of resilience, fulfilment of God's grace,
My breath finally, restored into place.

Poem 7. In Loving Memory of Dad

World full of chaos, my dad was my rock,
Through thick and thin, alone to never walk.

Alone in the darkness, a light shone bright,
Guiding us through, the toughest of fights.

A soldier by trade, a protector by heart,
Teaching strength, right from the start,

His love unwavering, his strength unmatched,
In his arms, all fears dispatched.

As a little girl, daughter's first love,
Daddy bear hugs, gift from above.

A role model, in awe of his might,
In his presence, everything felt just right.

Growing older, I saw the toll,

Battling enemies, ill body and soul,

Service related, a demon so cruel,
Trying to take him, you aren't a fool.

A natural hero, fought till the end,
Battling a foe, none can comprehend,

Holding his hand, watching last breath,
He'd fought bravely, even in death.

Reflecting back, on those precious days,
Seeing lessons, he taught in many ways.

Sacrificing for many, his love will always stay,
In my heart, forever and a day.

Butterfly kisses, my first love true,
Always in heart, whispering I love you.

A hero to many, lessons to guide,
In Father's arms, fears did subside.

Poem 8. Forgiveness

Forgiving you, despite the pain,
Despite words, leaving a stain.

Having no grudges, no animosity,
Trusting God's grace, all sincerity.

You've hurt me, you've caused pain,
Through Jesus, no longer strain.

Lifting you daily, I send a prayer,
Believing in Jesus, for needed repair.

Hurting people hurt, a vicious cycle indeed,
Through forgiveness, sowing a different seed.

Jesus forgave, I can't hold a grudge,
Release bitterness, the Lord is the judge.

I don't hate you, nor wish you ill,
Praying for you, God's goodwill.

May blessings pour, upon your life,
May the Lord bring, peace amidst your strife.

Poem 9. Blaze

Darkness of night,
Ready for flight.

A silent foe,
Ready to blow.

Flight suit a blaze,
An angel in the haze.

A comforting presence,
Holding no hesitance.

Caring for patients, day and night,
Nurse and medic, shining bright.

Flames and tears,
Bry calmed my fears.

Among chaos, she stood strong,
Her compassion, a soothing song.

Forever gracious, for her care,
That dark hour, easier to bare.

Let's continue, spreading love and light,
In this world, darkness can take flight.

Unity and compassion, the Lord our strength,
Together we can, go to any length.

Poem 10. Making Me New

A recognized hero, a uniform of grace,
A paramedic's heart, beating a steady pace.

Racing the clock, those in need,
Facing adversity, a selfless deed.

Winding streets, an ambulance flies,
Sirens echoing, symphony of cries.

Soaring above, helicopter in flight,
Aboard a patient, losing their fight.

Sights and sounds, lingering and haunting,
Emotions bottled, fear of taunting.

Twenty years, packed in the brain,
Twenty years, aiding others pain.

Screeching tires, a career to a halt,
The Lord closed a door, He's not to fault.

A new call to answer, in seminary I find,
Chaplaincy, new state of mind.

The Lord is good, He opened a door,
Blessings, upon blessings, He's about to pour.

Trusting His plan, it's all I can do,
Reflecting back, the Lord is making me new.

Poem 11. Sincere Apologies

Sincere apology, with or without cause,
We all walk about, with individual faux pas.

No hurtful words, should escape our lip,
Choose compassion, choose to flip

Don't concoct, spreading content of hate,
No violence, extremism a dangerous fate.

Bullying and harassment, can't be you and me,
Stand against injustice, tool of the enemy.

It's not flesh, inhabitants of the world,
Darkness it lurks, fallen angel hurled.

Praying peace, Lord healing every wound,
Praying wisdom, lessons coming soon.

The Lord, will protect us all,
In grace, Jesus breaks our fall.

This new year, trust the Lord,
Seek His face, guiding every accord.

Strive to be better, make amends,
Through the Lord Jesus, all transcends.

Poem 12. Parental Love

Parents gone, God gave me them,
In my heart, love will forever stem.

Daddy protects, mommy's embrace,
Their presence, never replace.

Parents' lessons, love and grace,
Despite wisdom, going my pace.

Raising children, no guide you see,
In children, love sets us free.

Guidance and love, always hold dear,
Biblical lessons, to forever revere.

Though gone, a legacy lives on,
In my heart, love that's never gone.

Word of God, forever I cling,
Losing my parents, a pain to sting.

Seeking and searching, Eternal Guide,
In His grace, always confide.

Parents gone, their love remains,
Every moment, His love sustains.

Poem 13. The Key

Once hating life, full of despair,
Something missing, completely unaware.

Filling a void, with worldly things,
None ever satisfied, it only stings.

Completely unhappy, lost in the dark,
A bright light, Jesus left His mark.

In suffering, He comes to thee,
His sacrifice sets us free.

No longer lost, no longer alone,
In His presence, a seed has grown.

Mending the broken heart,
Jesus gave a fresh start.

No longer filled with despair,
Jesus is always there.

To guide through the dark of night,
Jesus leads the path to light.

In His love, finding peace,
In His grace, worries cease.

Once hating life, now to see,
Jesus holding the key.

Poem 14. A Love So True

God gave me you, a blessing from above,
Knowing I needed you, my one true love.

Love to Uranus, love so far and wide,
Excited for our lives, side by side.

Through thick and thin, with God by our side,
We continue to stride, do not run and hide.

Thank you, for all that you do,
Thank you, for just being you.

Our journey together, a beautiful ride,
With God, conquering any tide.

Cherish every moment, every laugh and tear,
Together with God, we have nothing to fear.

Here's to us, with love so pure,
With God, our love will endure.

I thank God, for sending me you,
Matt you are my love so true.

Poem 15. In Loving Memory of Mom

Life with mom, journey filled with grace,
Moments, joy and sorrow, a tapestry we trace.

Hopelessness and despair, once clouded the days,
But a presence, illuminated the haze.

Deep conversations, a bond grew strong,
Your trust, a gift I cherished, a sacred song.

Life's storms raged, decisions weighed heavy,
His guidance a beacon, it kept us steady.

Calciphylaxis a battle, mom bravely faced,
Your spirit unbroken, your courage embraced.

Unbound by pain, that held you so tight,
In Jesus' embrace, you found eternal light.

A life not in vain, a legacy so profound,

For others have lived, your impact resounds.

No longer in agony, soul finds sweet release,
Resting in His arms, finding eternal peace.

If only you knew, lives you've touched,
Divine web woven, hearts you've clutched.

Your journey, testament, faith's enduring might,
Inspires walking, trusting, the Guiding Light.

In my heart, your memory will remain,
A constant reminder, our bond never wane.

For in your passing, a new chapter begun,
Your legacy shines, like the rising sun.

Poem 16. COVID

City by city, a mystery lurks,
Spreading fear, it silently works.

The symphony of life, it tries to silence,
Isolating anxiety, invoking violence.

World losing hope, enemy's icy hold,
Grief and despair, presence made bold.

Families torn, even further apart,
Masked angels, fighting with heart.

Exhausted and weary, finding no rest,
Obsessions present, in this cruel test.

Constant anxiety, a state of demise,
Enemy tool, a continued reprise.

Hope bleak, a light shines,
A beacon, through troubled times.

The Breath of Life, a solution so simple,
To heal the sick, restoring all people.

The world torn, chaos may reign,
Power of love, easing all pain.

Coming together, hand in hand,
Rebuilding together, in Christ we stand.

Poem 17. Burdens to Share

In silence, I constantly pray,
Blessings, pouring in every way.

Times of trials, too much despair,
Turning to God, our burdens to share.

Every trial, births a testimony,
His grace, it's not bologna.

In Him, all things possible,
His strength, a force unstoppable.

Pressing on, with faith and trust,
Love and mercy, they are truly just.

Moments in darkness, fears and doubt,
Nothing can hide; He shines throughout.

Through Him, a path made clear,
Burden light, no reason to fear.

Taking His hand, the storm rages,
To deeper water, the enemy wages.

Learning lessons, taking hand,
Trusting roads, divinely planned.

In the horizon, the colors we see,
Forever a promise, never broke by Thee.

Every storm must end, a promise of hope,
Living for the Lord, the best way to cope.

Intricate quilt, meticulously threaded,
Divine mercy, enemy dreaded.

In silence, I constantly pray,
Blessings, pouring in every way.

Times of trials, too much despair,
Turning to God, our burdens to share.

Poem 18. Endless Grace

The endless, expanse of time,
Moments converge, a tapestry sublime.

Drawing near, a whisper in the air,
Echoing truths, beyond our earthly care.

Hard to explain, the depths of this grace,
As we stand, before the Almighty's face.

Completely at peace, no need to fear,
In His presence, all doubts disappear.

With only one path, a victory awaits,
A triumph of the soul, beyond earthly fates.

Complete and total healing, a divine decree,
Willing to surrender, Mighty God's sovereignty.

His will be done, ever-present and true,
A different focus, a new life to ensue.

Every soul must declare, take a knee,
Jesus is the Son, sent by Thee.

Jesus the Son, the one and only way,
To meet God the Father, one eternal day.

Time marches, but in His embrace,
Finding solace, pouring endless grace.

Drawing near, the veil begins to part,
Revealing beauty, that dwells in each heart.

Hard to comprehend, this love so pure,
That transcends all, life forever sure.

Completely at peace, no need to fear,
For in His presence, all burdens disappear.

Regardless of the storm, a calm awaits,
A promise of restoration, beyond earthly fates.

Complete and total healing, a gift divine,
Praying alignment in lives, with the will Sublime.

God's will, a compass guiding our way,
This flesh, no longer focus today.

This soul must declare, Jesus, the one and only truth,
Road to the Father, the source of eternal youth.

Time, a river that flows without cease,
Drawing near, eternity of sacred peace.

Hard to explain, the depths of this grace,
As we stand, before the Almighty's face.

Completely at peace, no need to fear,
For in His presence, all doubts disappear.

Jesus the path, a victory awaits,
A recovered soul, beyond earthly fates.

Total healing, a divine decree,
Surrendering all, to God's sovereignty.

His will is the guiding light, ever-present and true,
This flesh no longer the focus, there's new life to ensue.

Time may pass, but in His embrace,
We find solace, a haven of endless grace.

Poem 19. Uncharted Path

Depths of life's winding maze,
Facing obstacles seeming to blaze.

Barriers that loom, unyielding and all,
Daunting us, challenging to stand tall.

Wisdom whispers, "Can't go under it,
Can't go over it, have to go through it."

Truth echoes, a call to embrace,
Discomfort leading to a higher place.

Growth stems, what's meant to destroy,
A paradox, both challenge and employ.

Pick up our cross, our burdens to bear,
Through Christ, all's possible, if we dare.

Arduous path, the journey so unclear,
In darkness, light beginning to appear.

"Get comfortable being uncomfortable," the voice
resounds,
For it is in this space that true strength is found.

Each step we take, each hurdle we face,
A testament, resilience and grace.

Ease of road, doesn't define our worth,
Courage to traverse, trials bring new birth.

Valleys and peaks, highs and lows,
Embrace discomfort, helps us grow.

Life's fiercest storms, forge our destiny,
Depend upon only, Jehovah Nissi.

Pressing on, faith as our guide,
Through Christ, we aren't denied.

For all things are possible, if you believe,
The end, our triumph, shall surely receive.

This journey, this path, difficult to tread,
Rewards await us, Christ replaces dread.

Poem 20. In the Right Place

Led to a church, a dark hour,
There, meeting, Holy Spirit power.

Grateful for family, found them there,
Bound only, by love and care.

Lifting up, when other's down,
Sorrow to joy, how profound.

Sing His praises, day and night,
In His presence, everything is right.

Thankful for family, holding near,
For in love, nothing to fear.

God knew, needing them most,
This church, home, finding my Host.

Continue walking, the path divine,
The body of Christ, for all time.

In their presence, sensing God's grace,
There's no doubt, in the right place.

Poem 21. Abundant Life

Depths of darkness, coming as light,
Guiding steps, shadows of night.

Always near, fear no gloom,
His presence, always room.

Life abundant, knowing you,
Pure love, so true.

In His arms, finding solace,
Jesus, forever flawless.

I am a child, belong to the Most High,
Jesus paid, we may never die.

Joy in the Lord, there's nothing else,
Worship and praise, He gave himself.

No earthly treasure can compare,
Jesus is King, always declare.

Walk in faith, not in fear,
The Savior, always near.

Trails, they come and go,
Peace, a whole new glow.

Thank you Lord, for all You do,
For your love, our lives renew.